Good For Me
Vegetables

Sally Hewitt

Notes for Teachers and Parents

Good for Me is a series of books that looks at ways of helping children to develop a positive approach to eating. You can use the books to help children make healthy choices about what they eat and drink as an important part of a healthy lifestyle.

Look for vegetables when you go shopping.
- Look at the different types of vegetable in your local supermarket.
- Read the ingredients on packets to see if the food contains vegetables.
- Buy something new. Have fun preparing it and eating it with children.

Talk about different food groups and how we need to eat a variety of food from each group every day.
- Vegetables are packed with vitamins and minerals and fibre.
- Talk about the ways vitamins, minerals and fibre help to keep us strong and healthy.

Talk about how we feel when we are healthy and the things we can do to help us to stay healthy.
- Eat food that is good for us.
- Drink plenty of water.
- Enjoy fresh air and exercise.
- Sleep well.

First published in 2007 by Wayland
This paperback edition published in 2010 by Wayland
Copyright © Wayland 2007
Wayland
338 Euston Road
London NW1 3BH

Wayland Australia
Level 17/207 Kent Street
Sydney NSW 2000

Produced by Tall Tree Ltd
Editor: Jon Richards
Designer: Ben Ruocco
Consultant: Sally Peters

British Library Cataloguing in Publication Data
Hewitt, Sally, 1949–
    Vegetables. – (Good for me)
    1. Vegetables – Juvenile literature 2. Vegetables in human
    nutrition – Juvenile literature 3. Health – Juvenile
    literature
    I. Title
    641.3'5

ISBN: 97807502561661

Printed in China
Wayland is a division of Hachette Children's Books.
an Hachette UK Company,
www.hachette.co.uk

Picture credits:

Cover top Corbis/Tim Pannell, bottom Dreamstime.com/Sasha Radosavljevic,
4 Alamy/The Anthony Blake Photo Library, 5 Dreamstime.com,
6 Alamy/Stock Connection Distribution, 7 Dreamstime.com/Paul Cowan,
8 Dreamstime.com/Sasha Radosavljevic, 9 Dreamstime.com,
10 Dreamstime.com, 11 Corbis, 12 Still Pictures/Sean Sprague,
13 Dreamstime.com/Dianne Maire, 14 Dreamstime.com, 15 Alamy/Keyfoto,
16 Alamy/allover photography, 17 Dreamstime.com/Florea Marius Catalin,
18 Alamy/Foodfolio, 19 Bubbles Photolibrary/Claire Camm, 20 centre
Dreamstime.com, bottom left Dreamstime.com, bottom middle
Dreamstime.com, bottom right Dreamstime.com/Andy Butler, 21 top middle
Dreamstime.com, centre left Dreamstime.com, upper centre
Alamy/Foodfolio, centre right Dreamstime.com/Lorelyn Medina, centre
Dreamstime.com/Andrei Dragut, bottom left Alamy/Foodfolio, bottom centre
Dreamstime.com/Olga Lyubkina, bottom right Dreamstime.com/Paul Cowan
23 Corbis/Tim Pannell

Contents

Good for me

Everyone needs to eat food and drink water to live, grow and be **healthy**. All the food we eat comes from animals and plants. Vegetables are food from plants.

We eat **roots**, stalks, leaves and the flowers of plants. Carrots are roots.

You can grow
vegetables in
a garden or
in a pot with
some soil
and water.

Vegetables are grown on farms and in pots
and gardens. They need rain and sunshine
to grow and ripen. Vegetables are delicious
to eat. They are good for you!

Healthy vegetables

Vegetables are full of **vitamins** and **minerals**. Every part of your body needs vitamins and minerals to be **healthy** and to fight **germs**.

Eating vegetables helps to keep you active.

You need to chew crunchy vegetables very well because they are full of **fibre**. Fibre is important. It helps your body get rid of unwanted food.

You should eat five **portions** of fresh vegetables and fruit every day.

Roots and bulbs

Roots and **bulbs** are the parts of plants that grow underground. They are large because this is where the plant stores the food it needs to grow. You can eat the roots and bulbs of many plants.

Carrots, potatoes, sweet potatoes, yams, parsnips, turnips and radishes are all root vegetables.

Onions grow in many layers
which you can see when
they are chopped up.

Onions and garlic are bulbs
with a strong taste. We use
them to flavour salads, soups
and stews. Be careful, chopping
onions can make you cry.

Lunch box

Ask an adult to warm
some vegetable soup.
Put it in a thermos
flask for lunch.

Leaves, flowers and fruit

Plants make food from sunlight in their green leaves. Cabbages, lettuces and spinach all grow leaves that we can eat.

Cauliflower really is a flower. We eat the white flower and not the leaves.

We often call cucumbers, tomatoes and peppers vegetables, but they are fruit. Fruit is the part of the plant where seeds are made.

Can you see the seeds inside peppers when they are cut open?

Lunch box

Vegetables have interesting shapes. Ask an adult to cut circles of raw sweet peppers to eat.

Growing vegetables

Vegetables grow all over the world, all
year round. Some types of vegetable
grow where it is warm and wet, others
grow where it is hot and dry.

Yams grow in
Central America
and the Caribbean
where it is hot
and sunny.

In mild countries, vegetables such as lettuces are grown in greenhouses all year round.

Vegetables grow in **greenhouses** whatever the weather. Inside a greenhouse, plants are given the water, sunlight and heat they need to grow.

Lunch box

Use different types of leaves, such as spinach and rocket, to make salads.

Buying and storing

Most vegetables should be kept cool and eaten soon after buying. Root vegetables should be stored in a dry, dark place. We buy fresh vegetables at a greengrocers, a market or a supermarket.

Fresh vegetables are delivered to supermarkets every day.

Vegetables can be frozen, canned or dried so that they last. Frozen vegetables stored in the freezer keep for about three months. Canned and dried vegetables will last for more than a year.

Canned vegetables are stored in water or juice to make them last.

Lunch box

If you run out of fresh vegetables, you can add canned carrots and green beans to your salad.

15

Raw vegetables

Brightly coloured raw vegetables are full of vitamins and minerals. The fresher they are, the more goodness there is inside them. Wash raw vegetables and chew them well.

Eating crunchy raw vegetables helps to keep your teeth healthy and strong.

This salad uses red, yellow and green vegetables.

You can make different coloured salads. Lettuce, green pepper and cucumber make a green salad. Tomatoes, sweet red pepper and radish make a red salad. Carrots and orange peppers make an orange salad.

Lunch box

See how many different colours you can have in the salads you make for your school lunch box.

Cooked vegetables

Vegetables can be cooked as well as raw. If vegetables are cooked too much they lose some of their goodness. Cooked vegetables should keep their fresh, bright colour.

Steamed vegetables, such as carrots and broccoli, should still be crunchy.

Root vegetables can be boiled and mashed, baked or roasted. The skins are good to eat if you scrub them clean.

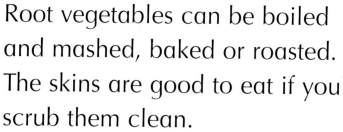

Lunch box

Ask an adult to roast thin slices of root vegetables with a sprinkle of olive oil and a little salt. Eat them instead of crisps.

Jacket potatoes are healthy, especially if you eat the skins.

Food chart

Here are some examples of food
that can be made using three
types of vegetables. Have you
tried any of these?

Potato

Baked potato   Mashed potato   Boiled potatoes

Carrots

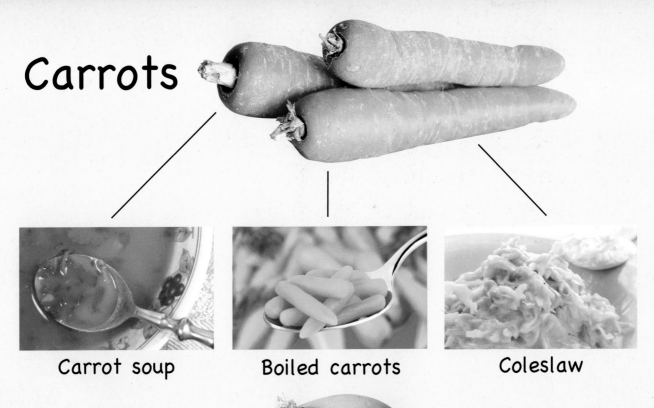

Carrot soup

Boiled carrots

Coleslaw

Onion

Onion quiche

Onion soup

Greek salad

A balanced diet

This chart shows you how much you can eat of each food group. The larger the area on the chart, the more of that food group you can eat. For example, you can eat a lot of fruit and vegetables, but only a little oil and sweets. Drink plenty of water every day, too.

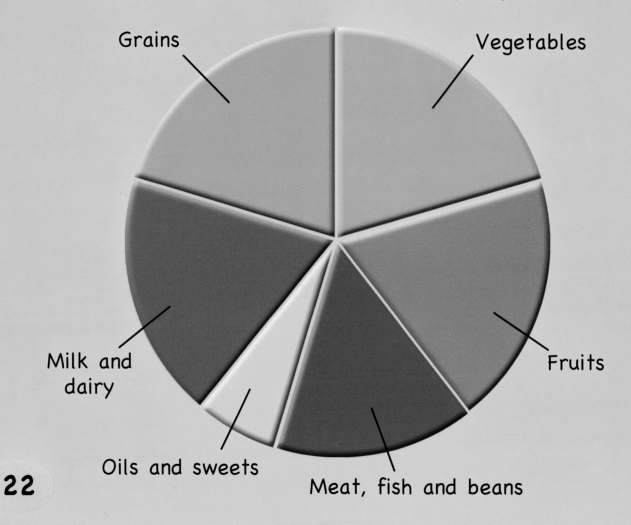

Grains

Vegetables

Milk and dairy

Fruits

Oils and sweets

Meat, fish and beans

Our bodies also need exercise to stay healthy. You should spend at least 20 minutes exercising every day so that your body stays fit and healthy.

Taking part in organised sports is a great way to stay fit.

Glossary

Bulbs The swollen parts of a root where some plants, such as onions, store the food they need to grow.

Fibre The rough part of fruit. It helps your body to get rid of any unwanted food.

Germs Tiny creatures that can be harmful and can make you ill.

Greenhouses Houses made of glass or plastic for growing plants that need sunshine, heat and protection from the weather.

Healthy When you are fit and not ill.

Minerals Important substances that are found in food. Calcium is a mineral that helps to build strong bones.

Portion This is the amount of food a person should eat.

Raw Not cooked.

Roots The part of a plant that grows beneath the ground.

Vitamins Substances found in food that help our bodies stay healthy. For example, vitamin D helps you to grow strong bones.

Index